The Book of Bearings

The Book of Bearings

DIANE GLANCY

CASCADE *Books* · Eugene, Oregon

THE BOOK OF BEARINGS

The Poiema Poetry Series

Cascade Books
An Imprint of Wipf and Stock Publishers
199 W. 8th Ave., Suite 3
Eugene, OR 97401

www.wipfandstock.com

PAPERBACK ISBN: 978-1-5326-7215-6
HARDCOVER ISBN: 978-1-5326-7216-3
EBOOK ISBN: 978-1-5326-7217-0

Cataloguing-in-Publication data:

Names: Glancy, Diane, author.

Title: The Book of Bearings / Diane Glancy.

Description: Eugene, OR: Cascade Books, 2018. | The Poiema Poetry Series.

Identifiers: ISBN 978-1-5326-7215-6 (paperback). | ISBN 978-1-5326-7216-3 (hardcover). | ISBN 978-1-5326-7217-0 (ebook).

Subjects: LCSH: American poetry—21st century.

Classification: PS3557 .L294 B55 2019 (paperback). | PS3557 (ebook).

Manufactured in the U.S.A.   01/10/19

Contents

Introduction

FINDING THE BEARINGS OF a book is difficult as finding the Geographic North from the Magnetic North, which are two different places. The Geographic North is under an ice cap. It is hard to stand on the North Pole without drifting somewhat with the drifting ice. Repositioning is required to remain over the Geographic North.

As the ice moves, you move with it, holding onto the pole you placed at the North Pole, and you have to move your pole back to the place it moved from. Otherwise you would be holding onto your pole that is no longer over the North Pole, but has drifted off center.

The Magnetic North, on the other hand, is not at the North Pole. Not only is it not, but it is moving also. Not on ice over a fixed place, but it moves because of the magnetic core of iron at the center of the earth, and the molten ore moving above that core under the earth's surface.

The Magnetic North resides somewhere in northern Canada, about 300 miles south of the Geographic North Pole. Though it is transient, it remains somewhat in the region, at present.

The same instabilities are in a book, especially if that book is poetry, which resides along the lines of the Polar Shift [the distance between the Geographic North and Magnetic North]. There is drifting between subject and connotation. Interpretations of moving fields moving across oppositions. The Geographic North and its annex, the Magnetic North. Their variance. Their alterity. Their swag.

The Book of Bearings

Variations in Magnetism

They would discover questions
the answers of which were magnetic variations.
They would take what was not theirs.
They would bring to the people unbearable suffering.
Their ships drove all over the water running into islands and reefs
trying to figure out the Magnetic North from the Geographic North.
All variables
though some hit and found their way.

A dead reckoning was only an estimate of changing distance
and changing course.
Currents and wind were other variables.
Even the iron nails in the wood could pull the ships off course.
Magnetic variation varied across the globe.
It changed over the years.
The compass was the ocean's language not caring
about the little ships upon it
tumbling them over in its waves.
Yet they hardly ever stayed at home.

The Book of Bearings

They fed us with stories of their world
that would include us
if we followed their God
who shuffled over those who would seek him
on other terms than his.
The harrowing.
The winnowing.
The changeableness of knowing.
In the meantime, the unused land is ours.
The animals their pelts and cries.

Chief Odysseus

. . .after Junipero Serra and the Legacies of the California Missions
Virginia Steele Scott Galleries
–The Huntington

He goes to another wife
they say of the sun when he disappears.
No, he goes hunting.
That's why the animals hide during the day
and come out at night when he is gone.
He makes the journey
like the dog chasing its tail it never can catch.

It is known the mission Indians have to be constrained
to remain Christian.
It is known they can still grind corn
with their feet in wooden hobbles.

Trying To Figure Out the World

In the beginning there was a boat made of bark.
Then a paddle
and wind on the current of the water.
The God of fury pumped air into the whales to enlarge them.
Always the large ones.
He hated to cut back.
But the expanding God had to consider shape and size
when they took over the ocean.
Deflate he wrote on his tablet to study.

We too made forays into other encampments
plundering the alphabet—
throwing letters against the wind
to see which ones survived.

We Played in the Sandbox Building Jamestown

The crossing was a voyage that absorbed us.
When we landed our ship
we began another passage.
We saw the savages.
Their walls and longhouses always on hilltops
from which distance could be seen.
They had platforms along the walls for weapons.
Their longhouses were upright structures
covered with bark.
They stood in rows with storage space
and outside the walls
their fields of corn beans squash.

We built our own barriers on which to post our cannons.
We molded walls.
Inside the walls we shaped block houses
with packed sand.
We marked rows for crops with twigs.
We had a few small stones for animals and a gate
from which we left with our muskets to hunt.

It was simple.
Build forts.
Plant crops.
Establish trade with the Indians.
Who could not thrive?
We built a little church and a glassworks.
We made a few barrels for tar.
The summer was hot.
The winter bitter.
The crops failed.
The animals scattered.
The Indians made war.
We suffered hunger, cold, diseases of the most putrid kind.

The next ship found us *Cryeinge owtt*
we are starved we are starved.
We were forced to eat *horses*
Doggs
Catts
Ratts
Myce
Vermin
Bootes or other leather
Starch in our ruffs.

Later ships found the walls of Jamestown *tourne downe, the portes open,*
the gates from the hinges, the church ruined and unfrequented,
empty howses. . .rent up and burnt. . .[1]

They found our sandbox where holes were poked
with twigs for graves.

---

1. Percy, George, "Trewe Relacyon," Governor and Council of Virginia to the Virginia Company of London, July 7, 1610

Homer[2]

A homer is a home run,
a pigeon returning—
if he would come back.
If there were children on the floor playing—
the bear might wear a hat,
the fox a glove.
She has garden scissors
for the spiderwort and stems without their blossoms.

2. 10 or 11 bushels

Garden Tools

They were there and then they were gone. You know this after long driving in a wilderness that could have been migration trail or settlement. The lifting of wind on the edge of soil—the feet of small animals burrowing—until a fragment of bone that could have been part of a small finger under sediment for centuries. The tone of wind blowing the soil—digging under edges covered with roots of scrub brush. The earth packed together. Until claws of animals digging and run-off of rain. Until the fragment uncovered. Voices of storms on the edge of wind turned back upon themselves. A narrative of time moving backward in space that falls into itself. Weight from clouds dropping. The rivulets washing into burrows—eroding. The bones scattered by scavengers not knowing where the rest was taken. A voice still there. The content of soil spilling particles of sand until the bone surfaced at last from a hill as rain working down uncovered the fragment that bore the marks of encounter—but survived.

Odysseus' Ship

. . .but if one went to them from the dead—Luke 16:30

The constellations are a garden—
their little flower-heads
planted after crossing the great unknown—

Their comets are dropped stones—
streams of dust and frozen gasses tied with string—
messages left by an unnamed ship.

Determining a Position

He sang the universe into being. His singing spawned reason, but not suf-
ficiently. So we shall never know all that moves within the universe.

> Kwaw Labors to Form a World
> Atsugewi, 1996
> Darryl Babe Wilson
> *Surviving Through the Days*
> Herbert W. Luthin
> University of California Press, 2002

No man can find out the world that God makes from the beginning to the end

> –Ecclesiastes 3:11

Learning to Write the Alphabet

My parents were in the cabin.
They were gone.
They came again.
They were gaudy.
The shiny spokes were from the window.
In a dream I ate beads from a dress made of buckskin.
The beads were fish.
They were berries.
They had lights in them.
I licked the light.
It was stars I mouthed in their glittering.
Their lone movement across the black sky.
Here a light bulb.
Here a hand saying, eat.
The beads from a string.
I picked the beads from the loose thread.
Little berries and shiny fish.
The voices were loud again.
Then they were gone.
It was light.
It was dark.
It was light again.
Would you like to live in the house with us?
Call us mother and father.
Learn sewing. Cooking. Washing. Prayer.
The yard full of children.

When Horses Weren't Looking

At one time the trees and horses were relatives.
There was a time when it was like that.

        –The Elders

I found a chair in the letter h
a small chair
the kind you sit in as a child for Bible lessons
with a doll
you could dress as a prophet.
It was what I heard in school
and what I heard at the house.
There were things that could be like another.
There were things that could not.
Would you like more tea?
The choice we were given always was there
in which to see their ways.

Bible Pages as a Mission

David came to Sheba's house at Jerusalem, and took the women, his concubines whom he had left to keep the house, and put them in a ward and fed them, but went not into them. So they were shut up until the day of their death

> −II Samuel 20:3

In a quiet house every move
is heard. We guard our cryings.
The turnings in our beds.
In darkness, our noises are judged.
We use them against one another.

The hours are little cakes to nibble.
Day and night without edges between them.
We lick our hands.
Sometimes ours fingers move
as if remembering.

I watch the light crawl into the window.
I try to stitch it to the floor. I hear its cries
as the stitches stretch. I draw the needle
tighter as it limps across the floor in pain
and disappears.

Register of Departures

They will carry at times
a heavy box.
Not one alone can carry it
but with all of them together
it can be done.

There will be times the box has no weight at all.
Other times it holds the ballast and a heavy cargo.
How glad to pick up the box
and repeat the journey that prints the letters
they will leave on the morrow.

The Water Blue from Sorrow

—we drive on without regrets through this desert where a fixed camp, however temporary, is frightening.

　　　　　-Simone de Beauvoir, *America Day by Day*

The earth is charred.
The edge of the hill is covered with ash.
The horse bites the air.
So many descriptions to hold it there.
I plug myself in for recharge.
I am horse and rider of the horse.
How is it possible? But all things are.
I drive the horse trail above the hills.
The horse loops and turns
capable of uncertainty
and all the encampments of the unknown.
I am thread in the horse barn.
The sewing machine turns out other horses made of felt
and stuffed with dryer lint
(and hooked to an electrical cord).
I myself feel I am reliable.
The narrator could be no other.
I run on two feet. Ride with four.
The stirrups. The saddle horn.
The leather sewn with large stitches.
Polished by use.

The Longing of All That Is Going

I saw a bin of pineapples in the market—
their rinds disrupted with mounds in rows all billowy with sails.
Not literal, but interpretation is the definition of our work.
The last stomp-dance at the outpost—
the pineapples with their hands held up
like children calling to lift them from the floor.
Maybe lined up with stars the way sailors, before the compass,
navigated in alignment with the constellations.
Maybe they landed with cranes and bulldozers aboard
for the impossible building—if only we had vocabulary.
Touch not the weary ones. Beat not their work for the day.

The Confessions of St. Bo-gast-ah at the Cherokee Female Seminary, Indian Territory, 1859–1864

To them that . . . are called to be saints–

    –I Corinthians 1:2

The Cherokee Male and Female Seminaries were boarding schools opened by the tribal government in 1851. The male school stood southwest of Tahlequah, Indian Territory, and its female counterpart north of Park Hill. Teachers were brought from Mount Holyoke, Yale, and Newton Theological Seminary in the east. Course list for females. Philosophy. Rhetoric. Composition. Math. Latin. Science. Geography. Music. Religion and Bible Studies.

The Female Seminary burned on Easter Sunday, 1887. The Male Seminary burned in 1888. Both were combined as the Northeastern Normal School in Tahlequah, Oklahoma in 1910, which became Northeastern State Teacher's College in 1921, Northeastern Oklahoma State University in 1974, and Northeastern State University in 1985.

The Female Seminary was a kingdom of learning. But mostly a kingdom of work.

The Confessions of St. Bo-gast-ah

Impossibly, we may live in time already past–
> –Dan Beachy-Quick,
> *Of Time and Timelessness in the Poetic Sentence*

I.

They spoke the world they knew, but it was not ours. They covered our world and turned us by force to theirs. We did not know how long the journey. Out of the barrenness, bramble would latch to the hem of our garments, coarse and brown.

Their words did not fit the land but scraped backwards. I sat at the school table looking at the marks they made for their words because their language needed posts to support it. I have thoughts they do not know. It's what I learned in their school. The boys mostly suffered more, denied hunting. In abandonment the stories crawled. They raked the ground for a place. They burrowed in what shape they could find.

Clouds appeared and funneled and disappeared and returned.

We scrubbed the floors of the room. We scrubbed the kettles of the kitchen. They were animals of the world that had come. I cleaned their soot. I spoke to them. I was quiet at night from the work. Once we burned a clearing to plant corn. Once we used fire to hollow a log for a canoe. Now our fires were in the stove. The kettles were animals of the fire.

The train stopped at the depot beside the water tower. Jesus died on a tree. Fire balls reigned in the night. The world they brought was fire. We didn't know where they were from.

II.

I read the words she spoke, and in the reading, she was again with a ruler tapping the table. I liked the parts that had water in them. I liked the wilderness of lightning. The jagged streams of light. I saw brambles coiling on the paper. Many more words passed like herds.

We brought with us our weightless speech. No letters marked its sound. It could pass through places their writing could not. It could pass through spaces no one could see.

In the garden, we planted along a string to keep the rows straight. The weapons of hoes and rakes were given to us. They said their words were everlasting. I saw our hands turning over new land.

The train came. I believed Christ. He was somewhere near. I opened my mouth. I saw the words she told me to say. It was called reading. I looked at the words until she told me what they said. It was similar to listening to birds speak. They with sound and form. The words were written by the shape of their letters. Lodge poles when the hides were taken down.

We could leave the treadle of the sewing machine. Where could we go? Back to the land we had come from? It was not there because we were not. Maybe it would be there again if we were. We had memory of it. That was our land. It was in our thoughts.

III.

They gave us beds that had to be made each day. We made our own beds. We made theirs. We cooked their food. We forgot who we were. They said we were no more.

They gave us *outings*. We entered their houses at the back and into their kitchen. We stirred their kettles. We were handed the plates after their eating.

There was a boy I saw at the kitchen table. He who did not take his eyes from his bowl. I spooned him more mush. He ate without looking. I saw him again going to the field while I swept the back step. He was wearing overalls.

The lowland fog was table linen on the morning cold.

We wrote numbers on the page like knives, forks, spoons placed on the table. The knife was a 9. The fork 5. The spoon 8. I don't know why. No, the knife was 1. The fork 4. The spoon 9.

IV.

Some of us ran and were brought back. Rufus Slab was one. His eyes on his bowl of mush. What did we want? To not do their fieldwork—To not take their clothes to the line. Ironing. Pressing. Sewing. Cooking. Scouring. Sweeping.

It was the upheaval that drove me to their words. In them was a place as if it were land. Why did I believe? It was because of lint I understood God. No, Jesus. It was hard to learn the names. The God. The Christ who also was Jesus. The lint of the believer. It was what I found when I turned the tub over after washing the sheets and clothing. Small clumps of it stayed on the ground as if growing there. God gathered up the lint from the laundry water and looked at its separation from what it had been part of.

Do not add to his words lest he rebuke you—[3] But I made words with writing. Words were one thing—and the writing of them another—when words lost their original place they struggled to find visible clothing in the alphabet. They were transformed to paper. They were objects. They were an occurrence instead of a momentum. That was what happened. I could wash and sew and see Rufus Slab in overalls who would have been a hunter or warrior. He was a buffalo plowing. Or a deer grazing in a pasture with cows who could not even know to step into the woods.

3. Proverbs 30:6

St. Bo-gast-ah Hears the Confession of the Deer

A train arrived.
The sky shone in the day.
The stars were pebbles we stepped across at night.
Sometimes we grazed on their light.
If it has to be this way.
If it has to be this.

St. Bo-gast-ah Hears the Confession of St. Ruth

Sit still, my daughter, until you know how the matter will fall–

—Ruth 3:18

The teacher unrolled the map above the chalk board in the classroom. With a long stick she pointed to the Dead Sea with Moab and Bethlehem on each side.

How did Ruth and her mother-in-law, Naomi, get from Moab to Bethlehem with the Dead Sea between them?
A journey of 7–10 days on foot depending on the route. North across the Jordan River.
Or south around the bulk of the Dead Sea, and then north to Bethlehem.
Women would not travel alone in the desert.
Did they join a caravan?
Did they travel at night to avoid being seen by robbers? Was there a marked travel route?
Wells of water along the way?
Did they ride a camel?
Donkey?
Were there tent encampments for rest either by day or night?
If they took the shorter northern route, how did they cross the Jordan River?
Was there a ferry?
A ford where the land on either side nearly touched?

The Jordan did not look wide on the map.
Maybe it parted for Ruth and her mother-in-law also.
Or was there a way they crossed the Dead Sea?
I lifted the heavy kettle on the wash stand.
I poured the heated water into it—loosening the mush stuck on the sides and bottom.
If you let the kettle soak after it is emptied, it would be easier.
If you let it dry, it is harder to clean.
Where you go I will follow.

The Dead Sea looked like mush from the kettle. No—the sea looked like
a blue gourd on the map with the stem of the Jordan River.

My arm up to my shoulder in the mushy water.
Swirling around the sides.
Feeling what is stuck there.
Asking it to let go.
Telling the iron kettle stories of Ruth who left her land
of Moab and followed her mother-in-law to Bethlehem.

St. Bo-gast-ah Hears the Confession of the Land

Now it is time to sweep.
A tree is a broom upside-down.
I think how they mixed domestic service
with a knowledge of Latin.
What could we do with philosophy? Religion?
All the words written on the barrenness.
The ownership of land was written words.
Even the land knew this.

St. Bo-gast-ah Hears the Confession of the Storm

I watched clouds from the window
when another storm came across the field.
We ran to the cellar behind the kitchen of the school.
A spirit was there hovering from the storm
more afraid than we were.
Its hands moved like a treadle while sewing
a straight line of thread into a fabric.
The storm became a large spirit trying to take back
its world and us in it.
Some cried. Others prayed.
The storm put on the garment of the wind.
I held the door closed with a rope.
The boys held it with me.
We had visions of arrows.
The lines were in the storm.
The words were rain and the rain was lines from the sky.
Then the wind was gone.
When the rain stopped, the smaller spirit was gone
from the cellar.
We went back to the classroom.
We opened our books.

St. Bo-gast-ah's Confession to God in Later Years

All this—the Lord made me understand in writing—

      -I Chronicles 28:19

It was a daily fog.
Sometimes I cannot get off the floor.
I am a slug that moves across the step
leaving a silver trail.
To know there was a bright light from within.
To know it even in the darkness.

Have mercy on the uprooted.
On the unwanted.
On the made-over to fit somehow.
You reform us, Lord.
You yourself were remade to a man struggling
on the cross.
You were thought odd.
You were dismissed.
In that we are one.

That Was There Like Something

Trestle Game

When I was a child they wrapped tree trunks
with bands of metal.
I don't know what they tried to keep from climbing—
squirrels or locust during a locust plague.
The reason did not survive the memory
of metal bands they nailed to trees.

I know the forces of war
are pushing again to stand.
They gain force with guillotines in their plans.
I wonder sometimes where they will be
and what catastrophe will allow their invasion.
Sometimes the trees would weep
beneath the bands.

I crawled under legs spread wide in the yard
when the children made a trestle bridge
and I the river crawling beneath them
while a train of unknown weight
passed above me as it crossed the gorge.

Flower-heads

A garden is a verb–

I don't plan on language saying what I want to say
but it will be the texture of flower-heads
under which stems are the conduit to the ground.
They can be parted with the hands
leaving a residue of pollen
pungent and sticky.
The tribes that wandered the plains
saw lightning crack the ground with its long tail.
The Indians, however, did not have flowers.
Nonetheless, when the air lit her sleeves on fire
she came to behead the flowers—
Zinnia
St. John's wort
Phlox
Nightshade
Snapdragon
Petunia
Foxglove.

Zinnia

The dentist wrapped a band of metal around my front tooth
when I fell and broke a corner.
It stuck out anyway—
is why it broke—
too many teeth in my mouth
or the mouth too small to hold the normal number of teeth.
Zinnias were my mother's flowers—
sturdy—
the hollyhocks from the farm would fall over in the wind
or else they had to be staked.
The petunias wilted in the heat.
It was a working flower—the zinnia.
As I would be a worker to get work done.
I felt their petals rise from my head.
My mother grieved at my ugliness.
I knew others would look away.
They would tell me stories not true
the days before caps and replacements
when roads were washboard
and laundry stood straight out on the line.

Father

Father wears a robe of yak hair
with horns pointed upward from his chair.
The arms and back and legs are carved from gopher wood.
He has a hundred jump-ropes he can jump.
His fleet has sails that are the eyes of fierce birds.
They follow ocean currents even in the worst gale.
He packs the ships with seeds for the New World.
He calls his believers to his holy land if they persevere through hardship.
Sometimes whales get in the way.
He doesn't leave his people if they drown.
See them at their own table off to the side?
I am that I am written on the Father's tie.
On winter days
the ocean looks like a gray table in need of sanding
but then the sun comes out
and sheens the water with a light that always has been there.
Father travels to foreign ports. He likes the crow's nest above the sea.
At the moment,
he has a splinter in his finger from stacking cordwood
behind his cabin where snow is to the windows
and he's out there keeping the path clear.
New martyrs are coming for supper
and they need a landing field.

Son

Son wears a breastplate made of thorns
and a trumpet vine around his neck.
It looks like a fox-stole someone's grandmother wore.
The tail of one fox in the teeth of the next,
or like the foxes Samson tied tail to tail with torches
to set the field of standing grain on fire.[4]
Son's legs are the river. His feet are swamps.
A name is written on his thigh: *I wept.*[5]
His arms are paved roads dry as toast.
No one disembarks but by him.
When Son is angry the water glares.
He was with his Father before the compass was set
on the deep,
before the mountains, the hills, the fields,
before Father made the inhabitable part of the earth.
He was instigation.
If canoes get lost among the whales
Son sends Father's ships on beating wings of wind.
Son carries a message that often is rejected—
I am the way.[6]
Son is flagman at the stock-car track
and flagman at the race of river boats.
He was with the Father when the world was set
with its engine running.

4. Judges 15:4–5
5. John 11:35
6. John 14:6

36

Childhood Memories

When God was young
his family was poor
flesh was the only crayon he had left
with paper peeled back like hangnails
he named his drawings, *people*
coloring arms and legs
the land shook like sheet metal when they walked
his fingers sweaty as he worked
waxy as a butcher
damp as bacon
but he was pure in mouth.

Holy Ghost

All their hosts shall fall down
                    −Isaiah 34:4

Holy Ghost wears furry chaps and a grapevine belt,
a red shirt and a cowboy hat.
He owns the marina by the river.
Hopscotch is his game.
But the clouds are his too.
Most days they are too heavy to let him off the ground.
He stays at the marina selling bait.
He sets a barrel fire to light Father's message.
He comforts the customers.
Holy Ghost prophesies for the Son's sake
with a string of words in another tongue.
He tells the Father's stories.
Comets full of ice once fell to earth and delivered the oceans
so Father could sail.
Their impact made the ocean beds.
The heavens are still falling.
Maple leaves splay on the walk like wrecked stars.

The Lord Spoke to the Fish—Jonah 2:10

I knew a whale in California who said it was a descendent of the great fish God prepared for Jonah. On the darkest nights when everyone felt alone, it told great stories of the great fish. Often, it would chuckle as it spoke of its ancestor. The young whales would honor it by not interrupting. The older whales would listen stoically. The whale said its ancestor was floating without purpose when God called it out for basic training. It would swallow a large air pocket that would bivouac a human-being until he was willing to continue his mission. It would even foreshadow Christ when he descended into the lower part of the earth three days and three nights between the cross and the resurrection.[7] The whale was to follow a ship bobbing in the theater of a storm. Even fish can see a tossing ship. There are storms underwater also. When whales jet to the depths and come up again, stirring storm warnings among the fish. But what did God say to the whale? That's what we asked. Was the great fish like the dog with a favorite toy in its mouth that won't let go no matter how hard you shake its head back and forth? Did God have to tap the throat of the great ancestor so it would vomit Jonah on the shore? Did it belch the air pocket also in which Jonah thrashed being a weeny who would moan to God about a gourd and the hot sun on his head more than the destruction of the great city of Nineveh?[8] Old stories are stored in the blubber and carried for centuries for nights that act as seats in an empty theater and pull the stories to them that have traveled down the generations like a row of whale bones on the shore with an unending trail back to Jonah who didn't want to obey God, but I ask you who does? The way on certain nights old men who have been soldiers talk of war when a loneliness rises from the brain and swallows them in the battle tucked inside the mind where missiles fly and burn the night air followed by the smell of sulfur across the wind. As maybe Jesus told his disciples he had been in the lower part of the earth when he saw them again on the road to Emmaus.[9] And how he understood Jonah in the whale after being there. And everyone wished they could hear the sound of the voice of God when he spoke to a great fish.

7. Jonah 2:1–7, Ephesians 4:9
8. Jonah 4:5-11
9. Luke 24:15

39

Stopped on The 5 North of San Diego

This catastrophe . . . can only be understood in the context of the time and its tools of navigation for finding a dead-reckoning position.

      –*Compass,* Alan Gurney

The end of them is never coming.
The brads holding them to their ships are not broken.
It was their frontiersmen that leveled the humming.
Wasn't then the only sheen of glare off windshields?
Here on the coast the ocean is more like Kansas
flat as a field of waving corn—the late afternoon sun glaring
off the shiny leaves.

Tooth

Prospero: . . . think'st it much to run upon the sharp wind of the north . . . to do me business in the veins o' th' earth when it is baked with frost

-The Tempest, Act One, scene 2

Stephano: I will supplant some of your teeth—

The Tempest, Act Three, scene 2

Did you know if you are silent long enough you hear the howl of the world?

I think there are cannibals on this island.

I believe the earth is round.

The last time I looked—no one came after me.

I am writing my own words. No one can take them. I hold them in my teeth.

I have no one to speak to except the migratory birds and whales spouting off shore.

Stay in that chair, the missionary said. If you get out of the chair—You will fall off the earth. You will be sent to an island.

When the missionary saw I was writing my own words—I was sent to the wash house. I was sent to the snow.

I believe a volcano is the cause of this island.
I do not believe Christ is the Savior of the world.
I see the waves coming like pages turning.
More than anything I want paper.

Alonso: Wound the loud winds, or with bemocked-at stab kill the still-closing waters—

The Tempest, Act Three, scene 3

Did you know there's an ivory carving of a tooth with a worm in it? The Inuit believed tooth decay was caused by a worm gnawing into the tooth.

Sometimes I hear a saw going back and forth—
Sometimes, I hear a cannibal hunting ice worms on the glacier. At night, I hear him chew.

Did you know the job of the first dental-assistant was to hold down the flailing patient?

The dentist put a wedge in my mouth to hold my teeth apart. I think he pulled as slow as he could to prolong the pain.

I wait for him in this dentist chair. He does not come back in the room—leaving me with cotton wads in the empty sockets.

These rages are helpful to me.

A tooth sits in a row with other teeth. Did you know a tooth is deaf?

Once a man left his wife in their cabin to go hunting. While he was gone, a bear tore off the roof of the cabin and ate his wife. Later, the hunter saw a tooth in a bear's scat.

I read my words to remember where I've been when one day is like the next. I cry and no one listens. I dance and no one looks.

Prospero: .. ... my ending in despair unless I be relieved by prayer—

The Tempest, Epilogue

I hear a volcano rumbling.
I feel my bones being chewed.

I believe Christ is the Savior of the world when my howls and the howls of the world are one.

The Northern Lights collide with the earth's magnetic field. They are a collision of charged particles along the field lines dragged by solar winds.

A corner of the ocean is caught in our pocket. We are dragging the world behind us.

I bear in my body the marks of the Lord Jesus—

Galatians 6:17

Did you know I howl at God's house?—When he has it closed up tight for the night, I sit at his window to let him know not everyone is warm.

Did you know sometimes the moon is thin as a tooth? Not even leftovers on its plate.

They came with their gasoline cans to the straw mattress of our beds.

We ride the ocean on our ice floe to an unknown destination. The walrus leads us.

Once this place was ours. Yet a storm brought others.

I'm sitting on top of the world. I'm showing my teeth.

Dead Reckoning

The process of calculating one's position by estimating the direction and distance traveled.

If Not Residential School Then Where to Go

Hindman Settlement School, Hindman, Kentucky, est. 1902

A dead animal on the logging road small and brown with fur it does not move it is stuck to the road

Its nose froze when the sun is up the ice melts enough it could pull away

A man touches it

It moves it is not dead its nose froze he loosens the way words stuck on the road is why you need punctuation to separate the clumps of words that walk on the road and stuck there

You were warned to leave the animals alone all of them they are wild

Wild thoughts do not leave they keep coming with fear that says they will hurt they will take when you are not looking if you do not look you will be taken

You stay in the woods you could hide if they came

We do not have roads though our paths stay the same we follow without a road and there is an animal stuck on the road is it dead poke with a stick there on the road it is stuck

Do not touch it is wild it lives in a world that lives with ours but we cannot bother its world

We cannot let thoughts run wherever they want they have to be killed skinned scraped with punctuation stretched to dry in paragraphs and worn against the cold

The ice stuck to the road that caught the animal that would get up but it froze the fur matted to the road it wanted to get up but could not until the man touched it and it was not dead

He loosened it for a moment it did not know it was not stuck it took a while for it to know it could run away

Stay where you are the man said give it a moment to know where it is to find the side of the woods where it can go

The rain on the roof is falling an encampment of words yet without marks to tell them where to stay what to say

The words in groups need marks after them they will teach you there you will like the pencil in your hand the sound of it writing on your paper like rain

You thought it was cold and it would be snow that does not sound like rain because snow is quiet it falls in the night but when the sun is up you see the white and it is snow

48

It melts and runs like rain it changes to something else it is not its own anymore do you want that to happen

They will change you from snow to rain or rain to snow whatever it is that is falling

They will hear your footsteps on the roof they will know you are the snow that walks silently and unseen until the light

Had the animal stopped to sleep on the road at night not caring it was on the road where a horse or wagon or truck could come

Only now it was a brown animal covered with fur that stuck in the ice that froze at night

The rain had stopped and was starting again it could hide and not be hidden by the part of it stuck to the road

Everything You Do Must Be Bible

Migration is an act of going—
a journey of the travel—
an act of receiving knowledge on the way.
Be in before the gate is closed.
Be gone before the flowers grow.
I feel their roots
raging at the window.
They long for flight.
I cover the bird bites on my arms
but there is a spigot and garden tools.

Dead Reckoning

There are flowers in the open air.
You'd think they wouldn't grow there
to function in uncertainty.
A navigational capability though there is no sea
unmoored
post-defeat.

.

Letter

If on a summer day you forgot your gun when you drove to the airport. If you had remained with us. You could have gone ahead to give your lecture. But you were one for leaving in your own way. After you made a structure of your words for us to talk about. Writing in your tablets there—the multi-rootedness of being. To stroke your way through the wilderness where you only thought you were lost. Maybe someone told you you were and you were not. But you could not stop to think—but intent on moving on—moved on. There is much going on here we could have talked about. You could have made more trails for the emblazoned mixed-blood undocumented academic Indian. There is stuff happening. You would have to face. But you also could drive off in your Land Cruiser to sacred places where the land tells its stories and you only have to listen. Our records are not missing there. You were not through writing your memories and the meaning of them. May your words continue to travel—bridging pitfalls. Blessed voyage. I would have turned the gun away from your chest and shot the floorboard of the truck. You would have had a hole where the road passes beneath your feet.

Choctaw Academy, 1825–45,
Scott County, Kentucky
National Register of Historic Places

The stone will cry out of the wall
   –Habakkuk 2:11

The choice given not to be
truant, to
serve, to labor, to
lose what was lived and live another way.

188 students—besides Choctaw—
Creek, Pottawatomie, Cherokee, Sac and
Fox, Ottawa, Miami, Quapaw,
Seminole, Osage.

They felt the hole in
their world but at school they would
be whole.
They were opposite words that sounded the same.
H-O-L-E. W-H-O-L-E.
One nothing one
all.

The boys felt the sheering of
their ways. Fleecing was a word like
fleeing, which
they wanted to do.

The school of dry-laid stone was
founded by Kentucky Baptist Mission
Society after all.

Other sheep I have not of this
fold. Them also I must bring—John 10:16.

After learning letters
they had to put the letters together
to make the words like
stones lifted
on a dry-laid wall.

Determining a Position

And he asked for a writing table, and wrote
      –Luke 1:63

An explanation of uploading
to the movers—

A box of puzzle pieces.
The picture of what the pieces make
is missing from the box lid.

Because the puzzle is old
pieces from other puzzles have gotten mixed in.
Some of the original pieces of the original puzzle are missing.

Now here is a wood pencil
yellow and stiff to mark the cargo on your list.

The Unwelcome News

From Philippians 3:10—the fellowship of his suffering

How do I explain the hard things to the sharp voices of the wind?
He came to earth. He talked to people. He died.
What had he said?—He was the Road. A place
we could not travel without him. He left us in a world
we're strangers to. He is with us though we can't see him.
He's working in another place with his hammer and nails—
making souvenirs for the tourist stands. These are our choices.
Rejection and suffering in a place the storm-winds blow,
or a trade we could unload. It doesn't make sense to anyone.
But for those who believe—the power of his suffering
would change a camp-ground of house-trailers into a row
of brush arbors on a desert highway where Indians sell their wares.

One Becoming the Other

Jeffrey Gibson, 2014–16 video, in which Natives talked to Native objects in a museum collection

The other coast was longer to get to as Franciscans came from Spain across ocean to forest, plain, plateau, mountain, rough roads through Mexico to another ocean on the west. 1749 Junipero Serra arrived [1607 was Jamestown] and 1769 sailed north to esablish the mission San Diego. The padres priests friars whatever they were called with their trappings of crosses against chupacabra [goat sucker], la llorona, mermaids. Their tabula rasa transposed the Indian to captivity.

The Indian eventually transposed the history of Franciscan arrival. Repurposed army blankets. Brass studs. Hub-caps. Speak to me dear Lord speak. Ceramic heads whispered another tongue. The metal twinings. Tin tobacco lids rolled into cones for dresses that jingled. Mud puddles. Mudheads. White headdresses notched as a mission church with goulash and succotash for supper.

21 missions up the coast from Basilica San Diego Alcala to San Francisco Solano de Sonoma. Hideous parades of clompings. The parades finally diminished to smaller clomps. Standing with objects unlocked in museum storage. Articles of deer hide. Sinew. Bone. Beadings. The Natives spoke to objects pulled from drawers resurrected with their voices.

Upon Arrival

You know it is a voyage you make. A forgetting that remembers what pulled toward it after losing. The change of happenings that blogged the continent. A changeableness of what is foregone. As ships went down to find their struggle to your world, you struggle to accommodate theirs. A conversion not of choice but a force recognized as arrival of what is to be there.

To cut with the past is to reconcile its passing with a different shape than you knew. It is listening to a radio station as you travel away from the transmission tower—farther and farther until nearly gone. You know it is ongoing. You just can't hear it any longer. And you have the visage of what you can no longer reach. You write about it not directly with the letters you have learned.

The act of assimilation tries to float on this new ocean. Covering the holes in your body. The tracings of another world on your bones.

Acknowledgments

American Poetry Review, Vol. 44, No. 6, November/December 2015, for "Learning to Write the Alphabet," "Childhood Memories," "The Water Blue from Sorrow," and "The Book of Bearings"

ANMLY 26 Anomaly (FKA Drunken Boat) for "We Played in the Sandbox Building Jamestown"

Bluestem for "Zinnia"

Caliban Online Journal #19, April 15, 2015, www.calibanonline.com for "The Confessions of St. Bo-gast-ah I-IV," "St. Bo-gast-ah hears the Confession of the Deer," "St. Bo-gast-ah Hears the Confession of the Land," "St. Bo-gast-ah Hears the Confession of the Storm," "St. Bo-gast-ah's Confession to God in Later Years"

Note for the St. Bo-gast-ah section—

I reviewed *Cherokee Sister, The Collected Writings of Catharine Brown, 1818–1823*, edited by Theresa Strouth Gual, University of Nebraska Press, 2014, for *Transmotion,* http://journals.kent.ac.uk/index.php/transmotion, a journal inspired by the Anishinaabe writer, Gerald Vizenor, and edited by James Mackay, David J. Carlson, David Stirrup, Laura Adams Weaver. Brown was a letter writer, diarist, and earliest native woman author who lived 1800–1823. She enrolled in the Brainerd Mission School and her letters reek with Christian vehemence. "Sometimes I feel the love of God in my heart, and feel as if I would be willing to give up everything in this world to Christ. O how good it is to enjoy the presence of God— Nov. 1, 1818." There were few insights into the reality of her life. I wanted to hear of the difficulty of learning a new language, of the rough transformation from orality into written text. It was a tremendous undoing of all that was known, and through it all, Brown wore a literary garment stiff with artificiality. Yet for her, it seemed to suffice. It was in Bo-gast-ah, an imaginary character, that I heard the trough of night that had to accompany assimilation.

Caliban Online Journal #34, January 15, 2019, for "Variations on Magnetism," "One Becoming the Other," "Homer," and "Dead Reckoning," with the accompanying piece, "Clothier"—I see these pieces as vessels for the black pages of the sea, which a book is. Otherwise the pages are left in their plainness—their starkness. These pieces migrate over unrelated terrain. The broken parts of it—little displacements aboard the rolling waves—clothing for the naked pages.

Choctaw University, Durant, Oklahoma, for a lecture and reading of "Choctaw Academy," September 19, 2017

De l'autre cote du chargrin, Anthologie de Poetesses Indiennes, Beatrice Machet, editor, Wallada, Avignon, France, 2018 for "Academie Choctaw, 1825-45, Conte de Scott, Kentucky, Registre national des lieux historiques" ("Choctaw Academy"), "Essayer d'imaginer le monde" ("Trying to Figure Out the World") and"Capitules" ("Flower-heads")

Facebook Posting of "Chief Odysseus," September 24, 2015, as part of protest of Pope Francis canonizing Junipero Serra

Green Mountains Review, Juan Felipe Herrara Issue, for "The Longing of All That Is Going"

Image, a Journal of Art, Faith, Mystery for "The Lord Spoke to the Fish"

Irises, The University of Canberra Vice-Chancellor's International Poetry Prize Anthology 2017 for "If Not Residential School Then Where to Go"

Louis Owens: Writing Land and Legacy, edited by Joe Lockard and A. Robert Lee, University of New Mexico Press, 2019, for "Letter"

Mount Hope for the section, "Tooth" Acknowledgment also to the Alaska Native Heritage Center, Anchorage, Alaska, for a video presentation w/ clay figures of "Tooth," January, 2012

Mud City Journal, Institute of American Indian Arts, for "Holy Ghost"

New England Review for "Trying to Figure Out the World" and "Flower-heads"

Poetry Society of Texas Summer Anthology 2018 for "Everything You Do Must Be Bible"

Potomac Review for "Son" and "Bible Pages as a Mission"

The Cossack Review for "Trestle Game"

Tusculum Review for "Garden Tools," "When Horses Weren't Looking" and "Upon Arrival"

Western Humanities Review for "Father" and "Everything You Do Must Be Bible"

Yawp, Bethel College, Newton, Kansas, for "The Unwelcome News," and for the 2016 reading/lecture there

The Poiema Poetry Series

COLLECTIONS IN THIS SERIES INCLUDE:

Six Sundays toward a Seventh by Sydney Lea
Epitaphs for the Journey by Paul Mariani
Within This Tree of Bones by Robert Siegel
Particular Scandals by Julie L. Moore
Gold by Barbara Crooker
A Word In My Mouth by Robert Cording
Say This Prayer into the Past by Paul Willis
Scape by Luci Shaw
Conspiracy of Light by D.S. Martin
Second Sky by Tania Runyan
Remembering Jesus by John Leax
What Cannot Be Fixed by Jill Pelaez Baumgaertner
Still Working It Out by Brad Davis
The Hatching of the Heart by Margo Swiss
Collage of Seoul by Jae Newman
Twisted Shapes of Light by William Jolliff
These Intricacies by David Harrity
Where the Sky Opens by Laurie Klein
True, False, None of the Above by Marjorie Maddox
The Turning Aside anthology edited by D.S. Martin
Falter by Marjorie Stelmach
Phases by Mischa Willett
Second Bloom by Anya Krugovoy Silver
Adam, Eve, & the Riders of the Apocalypse anthology edited by D.S. Martin
Your Twenty-First Century Prayer Life by Nathaniel Lee Hansen
Habitation of Wonder by Abigail Carroll
Ampersand by D.S. Martin
Full Worm Moon by Julie L. Moore
Ash & Embers by James A. Zoller
The Book of Kells by Barbara Crooker
Reaching Forever by Philip C. Kolin (forthcoming)

Made in the USA
Las Vegas, NV
23 January 2021

16432299R00042